SALT and LIGHT
POCKET GUIDES

COMING TO GRIPS WITH YOUR SEXUAL PAST

COMING TO GRIPS WITH
YOUR
SEXUAL
PAST

ERWIN W. LUTZER

MOODY PRESS
CHICAGO

ISBN: 0-8024-3504-1

1 2 3 4 5 6 7 Printing/VP/Year 95 94 93 92 91

Printed in the United States of America

Coming to Grips with
YOUR SEXUAL PAST

I hate him for what he did to me, but I'd marry him today if he asked me to!"

This eighteen-year-old girl had every right to loathe her pseudo lover, a married man who awakened her sexuality by his advances and seductions. He promised that she would be his sweetheart forever, so she felt secure with his affection. But when the affair was discovered he blamed everything on her, falsely accusing her of initiating this sexual liaison. She was betrayed and humiliated and asked to leave the church where they both attended.

Yet, incredibly, she was willing to risk everything and marry him, if only he would ask! Though he was married and the father of three children, this young Christian woman was willing to break up a marriage to have the affection of this man, the

5

first with whom she had had a sexual relationship.

This experience was so indelibly stamped on her soul that even the man's betrayal could not chisel him out of her heart. When she realized that he would not leave his wife and children for her, she sought fulfillment with other lovers, going from one man to another to satisfy her awakened longings for intimacy. Even if she didn't particularly enjoy these liaisons, she felt, in her words, "this is the price I have to pay to mean something to somebody."

Why can one immoral relationship begin a search for other sexual partners in a vain attempt to find fulfillment? This booklet is written to answer that question and others. *Your Sexual Past* will explain:

- The power of sexual sin
- The development of sexual addictions
- The doorway to sexual forgiveness and healing

Our sexuality is the most sensitive aspect of our personality. We are fundamentally sexual beings with deep inner needs that we are tempted to meet even at great risk. If we do not channel those desires correctly, we can embark on a destructive path filled with broken promises that will eventually lead us to a painful dead end.

Pornography is not the only doorway to the world of sexual brokenness, but it is one of the most popular. Young people who watch movies replete with various forms of sexuality often find their passions so stimulated that they want to act out everything they have seen. At least one-half of all high school students are sexually active before graduation. Any thought that AIDS might frighten them into maintaining their virginity till marriage seems ill-founded. Yet those who have sex before marriage jeopardize their chances for a happy relationship. (The reasons will be explained later.) This explains why we have so many sexual problems in marriages.

Then there are those who commit adultery or drift into the world of sexual aberrations. Acts of sadomasochism, transvestism, and homosexuality continue to increase, as those driven by sexual desires join the frantic quest for fulfillment with the right partner. Some are victims, suffering from the sexual aggression of others. Incredibly, one in four baby girls born this year will be sexually molested by a relative, neighbor, or trusted friend.[1]

Early in my ministry I would speak about the fulfillment and joy of sex. Now, after a few more years of

7

listening to marriage problems, I realize that for many people sex is not a positive experience. Some women who were molested as children find sex to be a difficult, if not a revolting, experience. At least a few have been raped, others talked into early sexual encounters that have had a devastating effect on their future relationships. And many people, driven by their sexual appetite, are sex addicts.

Sex can become the source of maximum fulfillment or maximum grief. A biblical understanding of sexuality will help us grasp the power of our sexuality. More important, the Bible can show us how to break the power of a destructive sexual past. Only God and His holy Scriptures can help people move from sexual slavery to sexual sanity.

Please commit yourself to reading this booklet to the end. Only when we understand the whys and wherefores of sexuality will we be able to appreciate the healing that Christ offers to all who come to Him in honest confession.

Christ can forgive and deliver those who are slaves to a sexual past. If He cannot, He has deceived us.

SEXUALITY AND CREATION

Think of it: Although Adam had the awesome privilege of walking

8

with God in the Garden of Eden, the Lord still said that something important was missing! "It is not good for the man to be alone; I will make him a helper suitable for him" (Genesis 2:18). God clearly affirms that man is a social creature and needs companionship that is "suitable" for him.

When God created Adam, He chose to use the dust of the ground for the raw material. "Then the Lord God formed man of the dust from the ground, and breathed into his nostrils the breath of life; and man became a living being" (Genesis 2:7).

We might expect that God would make a similar form of dust when He created Eve. But we read, "So the Lord God caused a deep sleep to fall upon the man, and he slept; then He took one of his ribs, and closed up the flesh at that place. And the Lord God fashioned into a woman the rib which He had taken from the man, and brought her to the man" (Genesis 2:21-22).

When God created Eve out of Adam's flesh, He made a powerful statement about our sexuality. God separated femininity out of masculinity, forming two separate people created in the image of God. With this separation came a powerful implanted desire in the male and the female to be reunited in an intimate oneness.

God gave Adam and Eve different characteristics. Men tend to be aggressive and depend upon a rational analysis of life's problems. Women have a strong sense of intuition, basic trust, and sensitivity. Obviously, these are generalizations and there is overlapping. The point is simply that both genders mirror different aspects of God on earth. Both sexes have the image of God, though they reflect God in a different way.

In marriage these characteristics are united in a harmony that should enhance man's representation of God. Paul taught that marriage should give a concrete display of the relationship between Christ and the church.

Here in the creation account are the roots of our sexual natures, proof that sex was created by God as an expression of unity and love between a man and a woman. We cannot ignore or misuse our sexual identity without serious consequences.

Two implications follow: (1) we must accept our sexual desires as from God, and (2) we should positively affirm our sexuality.

SEXUAL DESIRES ARE FROM GOD

All human beings have the desire for sexual intimacy. It is a yearning for completeness. The magnetic attraction between a man and a woman is innate, powerful, and unyielding.

God's entire plan for the human race was dependent on the sex drive inherent within every human being. If Adam had not been sexually attracted to Eve, the human race would have ended with the death of our two parents. But God made the desire for physical intimacy so strong that there was no chance that Adam would look at Eve and walk away!

The presence of an attractive member of the opposite sex, the fantasies of love that play in our mind, or just the activity of our sex glands without any external stimulation—any one of these can trigger desires for intimacy and sexual expression.

Of course, we are responsible for what we do with those involuntary sexual feelings. Both the Old Testament and the New give specific instruction on what sexual activity is permissible and what is not. Christ taught that when a man lusts (that is, sexually covets) a woman who is not his, he has already committed adultery in his heart. We are created with powerful natural forces of attraction that must be controlled.

This doesn't mean God wants everyone to marry. Some may desire marriage but have not found a suitable partner. Others may have the gift of celibacy, as evidently Paul had (1 Corinthians 7:7). Though the sex drive is powerful, no person need think that sex is necessary for either happiness or fulfillment. Many who are single testify to the contentment of their lifestyle. Others who are married may not be able to have sex because of physical disabilities or other mitigating factors.

It is not necessary to have sexual intercourse in order to accept our sexuality. Masculinity and femininity have their individual characteristics, drives, and aspirations. These must be accepted, whether married or single.

SEXUALITY SHOULD BE AFFIRMED

Most of us were raised with some necessary warnings about illicit sexual expression. But if this is all that we know about what God says on the subject, we will live with a sense of shame or at least embarrassment. The prohibitions of Scripture (such as "Thou shalt not commit adultery") are only one side of the coin; we also must understand God's intention in giving us these desires. We must strive to handle our sexuality in such a way that these desires will fulfill us and not destroy us.

Many Christian teenagers, wanting to live a pure moral life, think all sexual desires are shameful. They forget that to feel a powerful attraction to some member of the opposite sex is precisely what God intended. The very act of thanking God for such desires reminds us that our feelings are not a cause for shame but for joy. Our battle against lust actually increases when sexuality is viewed as "dirty." When we accept these desires in themselves as good, as God views them, we can be free to rejoice and to use them rightly, according to God's specifications.

To the ancient Jews, sex within marriage was properly considered a holy act. On his wedding night it was believed that a man actually went into the Holy of Holies when he made love to his wife. Let us not call unclean what God has called holy.

Let us celebrate our sexuality, rejoicing in God's creation. This will help us view our masculinity and femininity from God's perspective.

SEXUALITY AND MARRIAGE

What is marriage? In marriage, a man and a woman are joined by two bonds. The first is a covenant, an agreement that they will live together until "death does them part." The sex act creates the second bond that joins them in body, soul, and spirit.

Some Bible scholars teach that since sex bonds two people together, couples who have shared a bed are already married. According to this view, premarital sex does not exist, for sex equals marriage. This teaching has caused young people to get married, even to partners they neither loved nor respected. Their reasoning is clear: If they are already married in the sight of God, they should complete the union by having a formal wedding ceremony.

However, sexual intercourse of itself does not constitute marriage. A man and woman are made husband and wife by a covenant taken in the presence of God and witnesses. The Lord rebuked Israelite men for mistreating their wives and said to each one, "She is your companion and your wife by covenant" (Malachi 2:14). The covenant justifies the sexual relationship; the sexual relationship does not justify the covenant.

It is true the Bible does not mention the wedding ceremony (as we know it). But the bride and groom did enter into an agreement even if it was not ratified in the same way as we do today. Even in the case of Isaac and Rebekah, a covenant was made between Abraham (Isaac's father) and Laban (Rebekah's father). This agreement was spoken by Abraham's

14

servant (Genesis 24:48-49). Gifts were given to signify the betrothal.

As cultures change, so do the customs accompanying the wedding ceremony. But one thing is certain: A couple should not live together without the benefit of a solemn covenantal agreement. Sex binds two people together emotionally and spiritually, but the covenant comes first, establishing the permanent bond.

Today millions of couples are living together without the benefit of a marriage covenant. In most instances this arrangement serves as a back door of escape, just in case the relationship does not work out. But this arrangement communicates a confusing dual message. On the one hand the partners are saying to each other, "I love you so much I want to be sexually intimate with you." On the other hand the second message is, "I don't want to get too close to you so that I have the option of escaping in case you don't meet all of my needs." According to P. Roger Hillerstrom, "The result of this double message is an inbred lack of confidence in the relationship".[2] Understandably, these seeds of doubt bear bitter fruit later on.

Some ask, "What difference does a piece of paper make?" We answer with another question: "Would you purchase a house without a formal agreement?" Of course not. One reason for signing a piece of paper is to prevent one of the parties from backing out when a better deal comes along. Marriage, of course, is much more important than purchasing a house. There can be no security in the relationship without a formal covenant to seal the commitment.

To carry the analogy of purchasing a house one step further: After the papers are signed, you have the right to move into the new premises and enjoy them. After the marriage covenant, the couple now has the right to enjoy one another in the sexual relationship.

After the covenant comes the sexual bonding. Some think of this only as a physical bond, but if it were, sex would be only a biological experience (as the humanists affirm). But sex is much more than a physical experience; it actually bonds two persons— body, soul, and spirit. One person who bears the image of God stamps his personality upon the partner, who also bears the image of God.

Marriage reflects the plurality and unity of the Godhead. Though God exists in three persons, we read, "Hear, O Israel! The Lord is our God, the Lord is One!" (Deuteronomy 6:4). The same Hebrew word for one (*ehād*) is used for the marriage union, "and they shall become one flesh" (Genesis

16

2:24). Just as it is unthinkable that members of the Trinity would operate as separate entities, so a husband and wife should operate together with diversity within unity. The bond that has been formed involves the total personality of each partner; it is a unity with plurality.

Sex creates a "soul tie" between two people, forming the most intimate of all human relationships. When the Bible says, "Adam knew his wife" (King James version) the word *know* is not simply a euphemism for the sex act. Sexual intercourse actually consummates the highest form of human interpersonal communication and knowledge. Indeed this exclusive familiarity cannot be easily erased. Once a man and a woman have had sex together, nothing can ever be quite the same between them again. There simply is no such thing as a brand new beginning.

God intended that the first sexual experience be enjoyed by a man and a woman who are wholly committed to each other with the protection of a covenant. That was to assure the acceptance and unconditional love that guard the most intimate of all human relationships.

Once that bond has been established, it must be nurtured, strengthened, and kept pure. This takes place through mutual caring, and the development of trust and respect. When the commitment is threatened, the sexual fulfillment (at least on the part of one partner, if not both) is diminished.

SEXUALITY AND ALIEN BONDS

Unfortunately, our world is filled with people who have experienced alien, or sinful, bonds. Alien bonds occur when a man and woman are united sexually without a covenant of marriage.

Perhaps one of the most surprising passages in the New Testament regarding the nature of sexuality is found in Paul's words to the Corinthian church. "Do you not know that your bodies are members of Christ? Shall I then take away the members of Christ and make then members of a harlot? May it never be! Or do you not know that the one who joins himself to a harlot is one body with her? For he says, 'The two will become one flesh'" (1 Corinthians 6: 15-16).

We would all agree that sex with a prostitute is sex without a commitment, sex without any hint of mutual respect or caring. Prostitution is based on raw lust, sex for mutual exploitation. Yet, incredibly, Paul says that God joins the prostitute to her partner and the "two become one flesh." To prove it he quotes from Genesis 2:24, where God joins Adam and Eve into one in Eden. Sex of any kind always bonds people together, body, soul, and spirit.

Sex with a prostitute forms an alien bond, a bond outside the boundaries and nurture of a marriage covenant. This bond is an intruder, a violation of what God intended. Two persons have come together in an intimate union without the security of a covenant based on respect and trust.

A woman whose husband asked her forgiveness for his promiscuity said, "I feel as if all the other women he has had sex with are in bed there with me." In a sense she was right. AIDS researchers tell us that when we have a sexual relationship, we are, in effect, having sex with all the people our partner has had sex with. This is true medically, but it is also true metaphysically. Because sex joins people into one flesh, past bonds are still there.

What are some of the consequences of alien bonds?

THE POWER OF THE FIRST BOND

When the first sexual experience (or subsequent ones) occurs outside the marriage covenant, the sexual bond can be so powerful that it can even determine the direction of the person's sexual orientation. A boy recruited by an older male homosexual may initially hate the experience, but because sex bonds two people together, he may begin to feel a sense of security and fulfillment within this relationship. Soon he seeks out other partners, not because he was born a homosexual but because his initial experiences were so stamped upon his soul that he now follows the lead of his newly awakened desires.

This also explains why a young woman may marry a man with whom she has slept even though he may be abusive. His personality is indelibly imprinted on her mind and heart, and she feels an obligation to become his wife. Because of sex, he also may have incredible power over her. He may mistreat her, but she will always return to him. Even if the relationship ends, she will find it difficult to put him out of her mind.

Given the importance of the first sexual experience, we should not be surprised that some married partners are tempted to revert back to a previous sexual partner, often the first one with whom they had a relationship. Recently I received a letter from a woman who heard a message I gave at a couples' conference. Even though she was happily married to another man, she sought out a former boyfriend, her first sexual lover. The power of the previous relationship was still there.

20

Young people should take note: One reason to guard your virginity is that after the first bonding experience, something is lost that can never be regained. That special sexual relationship is best enjoyed within the bounds of the security and trust of a covenant.

THE TENDENCY TO PROMISCUITY

Once an alien sexual bond has been formed, there will be a desire to maintain that bond or seek other ones to replace it. Therefore one sexual experience outside marriage can begin a spiral of illicit relationships. Once a person has crossed a forbidden sexual barrier, he or she might have a powerful desire to do so again and again.

A young woman who was a virgin had a sexual relationship with her boyfriend in a moment of passion. After the romantic relationship ended (as they usually do), both of them began independently to seek a whole series of sexual encounters with different partners. When the girl got pregnant, she had no idea who the father of the child might be.

The first bond created a "soul tie" that could not be simply ignored. Thinking that sex was the doorway to love and acceptance, she pursued men with the vain hope that she would find the "right relationship."

A search for intimacy had developed that she tried to satisfy.

A man discovered on his wedding night that his wife was not a virgin. He became so angry that he vowed to "even the score." On their honeymoon he took a walk down the street and found a prostitute. Five years later he admitted that that one act had led to an addiction that he secretly nurtured three or four times a week. The power of one alien bond!

Today much is written about sexual addiction, but such slavery has existed from the beginning of time. Those who begin the pattern of alien bonding tend to continue it, seeking a fulfillment that of necessity will elude them. One writer said of sexual addicts, "They use sex like a drug, not to consummate loving relationships but rather to drown the pain of feeling empty inside a dark, shameful well of sexual oblivion."[3]

Individuals seldom have an abiding commitment to alien bonds. And because they have experienced intimacy outside the proper boundaries, they will have a tendency to forgo any process of courtship and almost immediately seek genital intimacy. Now that the principle of a covenant relationship has been violated, the temptation to continue the pattern will be persistent and powerful.

Many people are seeking love and acceptance through the sexual relationship, but of course, they do not find it there. A girl who did not have a warm relationship with her father will be tempted to seek love in the arms of other men. She is convinced that given enough time she will find the ultimate partner. Each time she says, "This will be different," but in the end it turns out to be the same failed relationship. The greater her guilt and emptiness the more she will be tempted to continue her hopeless search. She is looking for true love and acceptance in all the wrong places.

Admittedly, an alien bond won't always lead immediately to promiscuity. Some adulterers have been known to be faithful to their illicit partner. But remember that such a person has already violated his covenant with his spouse. Therefore, to violate his commitment to his illicit lover will not be difficult when the right time comes.

This explains why a man who commits immorality may lapse even after he has confessed his sin and turned to others for counsel. Sexual addicts, like alcoholics, tend to repeat their behavior patterns even after the most sincere attempt at reform. As we shall see, this cycle can indeed be broken, but the temptation will always be there. All sexual sins have their binding power. Some are addicted to pronography, voyeurism, homosexuality, or child molesting. Any one of us could become slaves to these sins if we just followed our lusts, wherever they may lead.

Those who know how to repent and come under the authority of one of God's representatives will find strength to form wholesome relationships; such a person can stop the strong impulse to repeat the same sin. Battles must be won a day at a time.

DIFFICULTY IN FORMING AN EXCLUSIVE BOND

Those who have had illicit bonds may find it difficult to form a meaningful permanent bond even within the security of a marriage covenant. Some will fear an exclusive bond, unsure that they will be able to honor such a commitment. Others find it difficult to focus on one relationship and cannot cope with the emptiness that past immorality generated in their lives. For some, past memories are so powerful that no present relationship can ever compare with the titillation they once had.

Those who come to marriage with many past sexual relationships usually will not form a strong new bond until God breaks the power of the previous ones. Time itself does not heal all wounds. The past must be confronted in the presence of God.

GUILT

Many people deny that guilt must accompany illicit sexual relationships, but because of the nature of sexuality, it is always present. God did not create us for alien bonds, and such relationships violate His will. Because sexuality is such a sensitive part of who we are as persons, a residue of guilt will surface in these relationships.

Suppressed guilt can rear its ugly head in many different ways. For some it becomes irritation and anger; for others it can turn into emptiness, frustration, or depression. Though there may be other causes of these negative emotions, repressed guilt is often the culprit. This guilt often plagues the conscience, quickens past memories, and stifles true joy.

Eventually the guilt turns to shame. Whereas guilt tells us we have *done* wrong, shame says we *are* wrong. Those feelings often hold people bound in self-hatred and condemnation. Often the roots of such feelings develop within a dysfunctional family, and are magnified through sexual misconduct. Some think they might as well commit suicide.

Young people may say to themselves, "Let's have this sexual relationship, then we will ask God to forgive us and we will start all over again. Everything will be just as it was before. After all, if God can't forgive us for this, what is the blood of Christ for?" Of course, God does forgive, but the power of the past experiences may still be there. But the same Christ who forgives is able to break the power of past behavior.

How can these bonds be broken? And what can be done in the lives of those who even now are plagued with past memories and addictions?

DEALING WITH A SEXUAL PAST

A Christian man who had a responsible position in a Christian school began an affair with a woman he met at church. Though his wife suspected his unfaithfulness, he denied it, even asserting, "If I am lying let God strike me dead!"

Because God did not take him up on his bold challenge, he felt comfortable in continuing the relationship. When he was unable to deny it any longer, he wept in repentance, asking forgiveness of both his wife and God. And yet despite his sincere attempts at reconciliation, he secretly continued the relationship, eventually leaving his wife for this other woman. To quote his words exactly, "I know I'm doing wrong, but I am helpless to do otherwise. I am driven to be with her no matter the cost."

At first we might conclude the man was not truly repentant. But remember, alien bonds often give partners incredible power over one another. This man simply could not find the strength to break the relationship. This woman could control him almost as she wished. Perhaps he had the same power over her. All rational considerations for his wife and children were tossed to the wind; all that he cared for was being with her. Never mind that after he got a divorce and married his adulterous lover, their new marriage ended in disaster.

In crossing the barrier into the forbidden world of illicit love, he was trapped by a power greater than his own strength. Little wonder the author of Proverbs warns a young man about prostitution and pessimistically predicts, "For her house sinks down to death, and her tracks lead to the dead; none who go to her return again, nor do they reach the paths of life" (Prov. 2:18-19).

Why didn't this man break his relationship? First, he was dishonest. Though he finally admitted his adulterous liason, he lied about the length of time the affair had continued. Despite his tears, his repenatance was only partial. Second, he was unwilling to become accountable to other members of the body of Christ. Because of his shame, he insisted that he "handle this alone." Third, he did not break the relationship completlely, but thought he could continue a "casual relationship" with the other woman.

Perhaps the primary reason this man returned to the same sin is a basic unwillingness to have God change him, finally and completely. The euphoria of his new-found relationship meant more to him than the will and desire of God. Thus Satan maintained a stronghold in his life that led to disaster.

Thankfully, God can help a man or woman come back from a life of immorality. There is hope on almost every page of the Bible.

There was a woman who was guilty of numerous illicit bonds, yet found emotional and spiritual wholeness through Christ's power. Women are sensitive and often feel the pain of immorality more deeply than men. The fact that she found a new identity and inner peace should encourage every person who is haunted by a sexual past.

Her story is recorded in Luke 7:36-50.

Simon was a Pharisee who threw a feast for Christ, wanting to check out this miracle worker for himself. In those days uninvited guests were welcome to attend as long as they sat along the wall of the room and did not expect to be seated at the table. Evidently this feast was well publicized, and perhaps a number of uninvited guests stopped by.

Among these was a woman who is described as "a sinner." Since all people are sinners, it is clear that Luke wants us to understand that this woman was a sinner of a special sort, namely, an immoral woman. Almost certainly she was a prostitute, a woman who was known to have many alien bonds.

How did she fall into such a lifestyle? Perhaps she was brought up in a good home and just decided that she needed to have her fling. One relationship led to another until she decided to sell her body to make some money. Also possible is that she was sexually abused when growing up and this led to an insatiable appetite for love and affection, so she turned to men for attention. Or maybe her husband betrayed her, creating deep anger. Thus she decided to take out her hostility against God and men by turning to prostitution. The men she hated could be used to earn a living, exacting as much payment as the market could bear.

Whatever the scenario, here was a woman with memories awash with the stain of illicit relationships. When she heard that Jesus would be in the house of Simon, she decided to be there at all cost.

The visitors were seated at a low table, perhaps a foot higher than the floor. In those days they would recline at such a table, each person leaning toward his left, propped up by his left arm and free to eat with his right hand. This woman, seeing Christ reclining at the table, went behind Him and took her vial of precious perfume and began to pour its contents on Christ's extended feet. As she did this, tears poured down her cheeks and in a moment Christ's feet were drenched. Then she wiped His feet with her hair. This act of devotion was done repeatedly, unashamedly.

This was too much for Simon. He was embarrassed, even if Christ was not. He said to himself, "If this man were a prophet He would know who and what sort of person this woman is who is touching Him, that she is a sinner" (7:39).

What an incredible story! Here is this woman in the presence of both

Christ and a Pharisee. Yet, here she found emotional wholeness. In the end, the Lord of Glory told her to "go in peace." What more could an immoral woman ask?

Emotional healing takes time. If you break an ankle, it takes several weeks or even months to heal. The healing of a broken heart takes even longer. But this woman moved through the process quickly. She did in a few moments what it takes some people months to do. She was ready for healing.

Let us notice several principles found in this passage that brought this ruined woman to a place of blessing and peace. She was honest, had faith, and confronted her feelings. We also should follow this pattern.

HONESTY

This woman had no time for hypocrisy or pretense. She had the reputation of being a sinner and evidently deserved it. She knew that coming to the house of a self-righteous Pharisee would elicit derision and scorn. To her, this did not matter because she overcame her natural inclination to hide in her shame. Her desire to meet Christ was more powerful than her desire to avoid public scorn. The insults that she experienced on the streets were nothing in comparison to the moral derision she would get from this arrogant bigot and his friends. Nevertheless, she was there.

Many people with a history of sexual experiences find neither power over their past nor strength for their future. One reason is because the power of their shame is stronger than their desire to be honest. As a result, sex addicts or those with a sordid sexual past often develop layers of denial. They virtually insulate themselves from who they really are and what they have done.

The grace of God does not enter closed doors but works only when deception gives way to honest exposure and humble admission of sin. Most people caught in sexual sin deny it, only admitting to what has been uncovered. This desire to hide allows the root of sin to remain intact.

The first step toward breaking the power of an immoral past is, in the words of another, "to die to the natural inclination to live a lie." God will do miracles for those who are so weary of their sinful secrets that they are prepared to "come clean" before God and all those whom they have wronged.

Those who are victims of other people's sins/crimes also must confront their past. Those molested as children, those who have been raped or otherwise abused, must be willing to face their past in the presence of Christ. Usually, the victim will need other qualified believers to be part of the healing process.

Don't even think you must change yourself to make yourself worthy of coming to Christ. Simply come as you are, openly, honestly, expectantly.

Step 1: Find at least one person (perhaps your pastor, a counselor, friend, or your mate) and share your past with him/her. Those who have addictions, emotional wounds, or guilt for past experiences need to be willing to share openly in the presence of God and those who can help. "He who conceals his transgressions will not prosper, but he who confesses and forsakes them will find compassion" (Proverbs 28:13).

FAITH

Christ said to her, "Your faith has saved you; go in peace" (7:50). Let me be clear: It was not her tears that saved her, nor the loving act of pouring expensive perfume on Christ's feet. Her good deeds did not bring the salvation of God to her soul. Faith, and faith alone, in Christ's forgiveness and salvation wiped her sins away.

But her kindness was an evidence of her faith. She believed that Christ would accept her even though He knew all about her past. Perhaps it was the kindness in Christ's face, or maybe she had listened to His messages of love and hope. Whatever, her faith blossomed in the presence of Christ. She knew this man would not use and then discard her as so many others had done.

How thankful she was that Christ was not a Pharisee! Imagine what would have happened if He had said to her, "Woman, I don't appreciate being touched by a prostitute, don't you know that I am the holy Son of God? Go back to the streets where you belong!" If He had spoken those words, her only option would have been suicide. For if she had been rejected by the only One qualified to forgive her, there was no other place in the universe where she might go to be forgiven. If the Son of God should turn His back, there is but eternal despair. But if He should speak a word of forgiveness, there is eternal joy!

A young woman wrote me saying that an older woman in her office convinced her that they should have sex together. Although initially resistant, she gave in, and thus began a five-year struggle with lesbianism (female homosexuality). "Oh, how I stink in the core of my being!" she wrote. "I know God has forgiven me, but I cannot forgive myself. Many times I cannot help but cry. . . at twenty-five I feel so tired and old. God forbid that I should be a Judas, who felt sorry for what he had done, but nevertheless chose to go in the wrong direction! Is there any hope for someone like me?"

Yes! A thousand times yes, there is hope.

But why does she still feel defiled though she has confessed her sins, perhaps many times? First, she must not only claim God's forgiveness but also His cleansing, which is her right. Her conscience can be wiped clean, and she can live without the voices of condemnation, without the heaviness that comes with a defiled conscience.

Second, she may be making the error of confusing the accusations of the devil with the voice of the Holy Spirit. The responsibility of the Holy Spirit is to convict us of sin so that we might confess it. After that the work of the Spirit ends. But at this point Satan usually takes over and tries to imitate the work of God and convict us of sins that God has already forgiven! Believers who think the accusations of the devil are the convictions of the Spirit are caught in a vicious cycle—they engage in continual confession without the assurance of forgiveness. Or they believe the lie that they must live with guilt as a payment for sin.

Forgiveness and cleansing are available for all sins. "If we confess our sins, He is faithful and righteous to forgive us our sins and to cleanse us from all unrighteousness" (1 John 1:9). When Christ died on the cross, His death was a payment for the sins of immorality committed by His children. Why should anyone think that he/she must pay a second time by wallowing in guilt? If you have confessed your sin, the next time Satan reminds you of your past remind him of his future!

If a prostitute can be cleansed in the presence of Christ 2,000 years ago, a lesbian can be cleansed today. Both can hear the voice of the Savior, "Your faith has saved you; go in peace."

Step 2: Accept God's Word that Christ's death was a full and complete payment for your sin. Repent, and be willing to accept the forgiveness that God freely offers. "I, even I, am the one who wipes out your transgressions for my own sake; and I will not remember your sins" (Isaiah 43:25).

FACING THE PAIN

This woman wept. She wept profusely. Her tears ran down her cheeks and fell onto Christ's feet. The present tense of the verbs indicates that she *kept on* weeping, *kept on* anointing His feet, *kept on* wiping His feet with her hair. Her tears proved that she was willing to face her pain; she faced the hurts buried in her sordid past.

Why did she weep? We cannot know, but we can surmise the reasons. First, think of the men who betrayed her! The broken promises, the assurances of protection and love. Then after they used her, she was tossed aside like the peelings of an orange. She was stripped of all sense of value and self-worth.

Second, she may have wept because of the grief of broken relationships. Perhaps she met a married man whom she dearly loved, yet knew that this friendship would have to be permanently broken. Those who are in alien bonds must understand that breaking such relationships sometimes involves the same emotional loss as the death of a spouse. Perhaps she was in mourning.

Third, she may have been weeping because she remembered a family that had been broken by her own sin. She may have been thinking of a sexual relationship with a married man whose marriage came apart because of the relationship. She remembered the little children deprived of the security of a happy father and a mother, and she was an accomplice in it all. Weep she might!

She could have taken all of these feelings and stuffed them deep within her soul, unwilling to face the pain of the past. Then she would have become a tough woman, defiant and angry. She could have told herself, "I will handle my pain and manage my life quite well on my own. I will not let my feelings get to me, no matter the cost!"

Or she could have pursued continuous compulsive sex to deaden the pain of an empty life. She could have continued to flit from one relationship to another, unwilling to admit the fruitlessness of her search for love and acceptance.

Almost every person struggling with a history of sexual brokenness has a moment of truth, a time when he/she finally is willing to confront the pain that has been pushed down in the depths of the soul. For every alien bond there is at least one hurting heart.

I do not mean to imply that we cannot be forgiven unless we weep; nor do I want to imply that her tears paid for her misdeeds. But sexual sin almost always involves deep pain that is buried in the bottom of the soul. Because many addictions have their roots in a dysfunctional family, only through a willingness to confront pain does healing take place.

Victims of abuse must especially be willing to weep. It is said that children who have been abused have "no place in the depths of their soul where they may cry their eyes out." Whether you suffer from sins done against you or sins that you have committed, pain lives in the depths of your soul. If you have never confronted it, weep in the presence of Christ. Tears are not only permissible but welcome.

Step 3: Ask God to reveal any areas of pain that you have ignored because of denial or a basic unwillingness to admit how deeply you have been hurt or have hurt others. Confront the pain in the presence of Christ and a trusted counselor.

ACCEPTING FORGIVENESS

Christ used the occasion to give Simon a lesson in forgiveness. "A certain money lender had two debtors; one owed five hundred denarii, and the other fifty. When they were unable to repay, he graciously forgave them both. Which of them therefore will love him the more?" Simon answered and said, "I suppose the one whom he forgave more." And He said to him, "You have judged correctly" (vv. 41-43).

Then Christ made His point: He reminded Simon, "Do you see this woman? I entered your house; you gave Me no water for My feet, but she has wet my feet with her tears, and wiped them with her hair. You gave me no kiss; but she, since the time I came in, has not ceased to wipe my feet. You did not anoint my head with oil, but she anointed My feet with perfume. For this reason I say to you, her sins, which are many, have been forgiven, for she loved much; but he who is forgiven little, loves little" (vv. 44-47).

Christ taught that the degree of our love depended on the degree of our forgiveness. Of course this should not be interpreted to mean that Simon could never love Christ deeply because he had but few sins that needed forgiveness. Christ's intent was to teach that those who *think* they need little forgiveness love only little. Those who see their sin with clearer eyes will love much.

To this woman who in humility saw herself for what she was, Christ said, "Your sins have been forgiven" (v. 48). Right in the presence of this self-righteous, judgmental bigot Christ publicly declared this woman forgiven! Perhaps for the first time in years someone actually spoke to her in kindness; someone gave her the dignity of letting those around her know that she was special to God. What blessed words, "You are forgiven"!

I have counseled many people who committed sexual sins who simply could not receive God's forgiveness. Some thought it didn't seem right that they should be cleansed because they were keenly aware that they didn't deserve it. Of course, no one deserves it! Forgiveness is a free gift based upon the merit of Christ. That's why God does not find it more difficult to forgive big sins than He does small ones!

Others find it difficult to accept forgiveness because they confuse a clear conscience with the consequences of sin. In other words, because the consequences of their sins continue (a broken relationship, a pregnancy, a sexually transmitted disease, etc.) they think they are not entitled to a clear conscience. But let me emphasize: *It is God's will that you be totally cleared of the guilt of your sin regardless of the awful consequences it produced.* If David could be forgiven for adultery and killing Uriah (who would never be raised back to life), why cannot others be forgiven of a sexual sin despite its consequences?

Still others cannot forgive themselves. But think about this for a moment: If the Supreme Lawgiver of the Universe has pronounced you clean, do you have the right to pronounce yourself dirty? "Who shall bring a charge against God's elect? God is the one who justifies; who is the one who condemns? Christ Jesus is He who died, yes, rather who was raised, who is at the right hand of God, who also intercedes for us" (Romans 8:33-34).

Resist the temptation to come to Christ with something in your hand, some promise of reform, some act of kindness you have done either past or present. Accept His forgiveness just as you are.

Christ is not physically present on earth to tell us "Your sins are forgiven." But through His Word, we can say exactly those words to those who have confessed their sins. Sometimes I personally have given people that assurance on the basis of Scripture.

Must you live with remorse? No, for remorse is simply repentance made out of sight of Christ. Standing before Him, the past is wiped away.

Step 4: Praise God for His forgiveness regardless of your past! Accept a clear conscience and the cleansing that is your right as a child of God. Rather than repeatedly confessing your sin, affirm the fact that you have been forgiven (Psalm 32:1-2).

Christ's final words to this woman were "Go in peace" (v. 50).

In another account we read that the Pharisees brought to Christ a woman who was found in adultery. They asked Christ what to do with her, reminding Him that the law commanded that such should be stoned. He agreed that they could go ahead and stone her, but He requested that the person among them who was without sin (that is, the person who is free of the same sin they accused her of) should cast the first stone. Pierced by their own consciences, the men all walked away, leaving only Christ and the woman. Christ's response: "Neither do I condemn you; go your way. From now on sin no more" (John 8:11).

"Go and sin no more!" Break those sinful relationships that keep causing you to sin! Now that you have come to Christ and received His forgiveness, you must take these additional steps to lay your past to rest.

First, if you have been wronged, you must *choose to forgive all who have mistreated you*. This may take time, but it must be done by an act of the will and with the power of God. Resist any tendency to retain your anger because you crave justice. Your desire for justice is legitimate, but you must wholly give your com-

43

plaint to God. "Never take your own revenge, beloved, but leave room for the wrath of God, for it is written, 'Vengeance is Mine, I will repay,' says the Lord" (Romans 12:19).

Yes, you must repent of any bitterness toward God or others. Despite the sins of your parents or those who have taken advantage of you, you must forgive. Daughters who have been molested by their fathers, young women who have been raped by their boyfriends, women whose husbands have been unfaithful— these and others must release the feelings of bitterness to God. Often the chains of past bonds are strengthened by feelings of bitterness and hostility.

Second, *become accountable to someone who will stand with you* in breaking sinful relationships or habits. Christ, when speaking of adultery and lust, said, "And if your right eye makes you stumble, tear it out and throw it from you; for it is better for you that one of the parts of your body perish, than for your whole body to be thrown into hell" (Matthew 5:30). Obviously it would be painful to have our right eye plucked out, but Christ is saying, 'Do anything necessary to keep you from sliding into the pit of sexual sin.' If it means breaking a relationship with a lover, *do it*. Burn the bridges that lead to your weakness, your addiction. Accept the pain such an act requires as your opportunity to prove that you love God supremely.

Third, *believe the Word of God and not your conscience, memory, or emotions.* If you are a believer, you are in Christ seated above all principalities and powers. You are not an adulterer, homosexual, or a rejected child. You are a child of the king, with all rights and privileges pertaining to such honor (1 Corinthians 6:11). Memorize Scripture that speaks of your position in Christ. "You shall know the truth, and the truth shall make you free" (John 8:32).

Fourth, *accept the power of the Holy Spirit,* who is given to believers. Through faith receive His strength, which can bring emotional wholeness to any needy heart. The destructive memories of the past can be replaced by: love, joy, peace, patience, kindness, goodness, faithfulness, gentleness, and self-control (Galatians 5:22-23).

Fifth, *become acquainted with "spiritual warfare."* That is, learn to resist Satan and enlist others who will pray against his power. Stand on the fact that you have been joined to Christ in His death, resurrection, and ascension (Romans 6:1-18). Expect to be tempted to return to the sin of which you have repented. Remember, we will always be tempted to return to the sin that once was our master.

As we have learned, in one sense, a person who has committed sexual sin cannot begin over again. But spiritually it is possible to have a new beginning. When Hosea's wife drifted from one lover to another, he said that one day he would win her back, and she would sing again, as in the days of her youth. "And I will betroth you to Me in righteousness and in justice, in lovingkindness and in compassion, and I will betroth you to Me in faithfulness. Then you will know the Lord" (Hosea 2:19-20).

What Hosea did for his wayward wife, God does for His wayward people today.

Charles Wesley understood that many people whose sin has been canceled by God still come under its power. But he assures us:

> He breaks the power of canceled sin,
> He sets the prisoner free;
> His blood can make the foulest clean;
> His blood availed for me.[4]

Once plagued by their sexual pasts, thousands of people are walking in freedom today, thanks to the power of Christ's blood.

What happened in the past can never be changed. But the power of that past can be laid to rest by the power of forgiveness through the Cross. "Where sin abounds, grace abounds much more" (Romans 5:20).

Notes

1. This figure, commonly reported in the news media, may be low. In a recent study, John Powell at Michigan State University reported that 38 percent of women interviewed had been sexually abused by an adult or family member by age eighteen (as reported in Dan Allender, *The Wounded Heart* [Colorado Springs: NavPress, 1990], back cover).
2. P. Roger Hillerstrom, *Intimate Deception* (Portland: Multnomah, 1989), p. 30.
3. Michael Castleman, "Addicted to Love," *Chicago Tribune*, Style, January 30, 1991, p. 6.
4. "O for a Thousand Tongues to Sing," verse 3.